D0777381

every teenager's
little black book
on cash

by blaine bartel

every teenager's
little black book
on cash

by blaine bartel

Harrison House
Tulsa, Oklahoma

06 05 04 03 02   10 9 8 7 6 5 4 3 2 1

Every Teenager's Little Black Book on Cash
ISBN 1-57794-458-5
Copyright © 2002 by Blaine Bartel
PO Box 691923
Tulsa, Oklahoma 74179

Published by Harrison House, Inc.
P.O. Box 35035
Tulsa, Oklahoma 74153

contents

contents (continued)

The Rewards of Work

Become a Money Channel

contents (continued)

Who Wants To Be a Millionaire?

Budget, Plan, and Prosper

ENTRY

[LOVE IS NOT FOR SALE]

5 WAYS MONEY CAN DESTROY PEOPLE

Movies, and most other media, paint the picture that money is the solution to all your problems. "If you have more money, everything will be better." That is not true. In fact, money, if handled and perceived incorrectly, can destroy people. Here are 5 ways money can destroy in the hands of the wrong person.

1. Money can give a false sense of security. Jesus rebuked the church of Laodicea in Revelation 3:17 because they were cold toward Him, thinking they were okay because they had wealth.

2. Money can cause people to worry about a need for more. Jesus said that our lives do not consist in the abundance of our possessions. (Luke 12:15.)

3. Some people in their greed for more money will compromise to gain. What they compromise to gain, they will have to compromise to keep; but they will eventually lose it all. (Prov. 13:11.)

4. When people have money, they often worry about losing it. The money they thought would give peace of mind now enslaves them to fear.

5. Love of money can choke God's Word from being fruit-
    ful in our lives. (Matt. 13:22.)

Money isn't a bad thing. In fact, it can prove to be a powerful tool for good in the hands of the right person. Make sure you aren't destroyed by the 5 misconceptions of money.

3 REASONS PEOPLE ARE
MORE IMPORTANT THAN CASH

It's sad, but some people find out too late in life that people are more important than money. They spend their whole lives pursuing an inanimate object that can't live, love, or laugh. In their passionate pursuit, they ignore and neglect their loved ones. When they grow old, they find themselves wealthy but alone. None of their kids or grandkids visit them. Their spouses, tired of neglect, have left them.

Don't get to the end of your life and find yourself all alone. Money is a poor comfort. Here are 3 reasons people are more important in your life than money.

1. You can take people with you to heaven, but your money stays here. People are eternal spirits whom you can lead to Christ and spend eternity with. Money wastes away.

2. People will love you, but money cannot. You can't buy love, and money can't replace the fulfillment that comes from being loved by people.

3. People can comfort you when you're ill, but money can only buy doctors. Friends can encourage you and laugh and cry with you, and they won't bill you for it.

Don't neglect the important relationships in your life for money or you might one day find yourself alone.

4 PRIORITY CHECKUPS YOU CAN DO

Take this little test to see if you are balanced in your views of money.

		YES	NO
1.	When you're undercharged $20 at the store, do you return the extra money?	☐	☐
2.	You see someone drop their wallet. You open it to find $500 cash. Do you quickly flag the person down to return it?	☐	☐
3.	When you receive any money, do you always set 10 percent aside for God? Are you excited to bring it to church and give Him your tithes?	☐	☐
4.	You see a friend in a financial crisis and you feel a prompt in your heart to give him or her your last $25. Do you do it?	☐	☐

Total your "yes" and "no" answers and rate how you handle money. Four "yes" answers: you're doing great. Three "yes" answers: you are on your way to financial greatness—keep improving. Two "yes" answers: your character with money is weak; your financial future isn't looking too bright. One "yes" answer: keep your day job; you're taking a tough financial road. Zero "yes" answers: you're a scrooge and on a highway to poverty.

6 ATTRIBUTES OF REAL LOVE

You can't buy love, and you can't replace love with money. What many people call love is really "lust." Read 1 Corinthians 13 to discover the true definition of love. Here is a quick summary of 6 attributes of real love.

1. **Love gives with no strings attached.** Some people give nice gifts but attach strings. Real love gives expecting nothing in return.

2. **Love looks for what it can give rather than what it can get.** This perspective would change 99 percent of American relationships. Do you see people as opportunities to gain something for yourself or as an opportunity to give?

3. **Love is quick to forgive.** It doesn't keep a running tab of past offenses. Freely God has forgiven us; freely we should forgive others. (Matt. 10:8.)

4. **Love is patient.** This is tough in today's "must-have-it-now," drive-up-window society. But love is patient with others because God is patient with us.

5. **Love has a humble heart and attitude.** Real love knows that anything good we have is because of God's goodness in our lives. We can't take the credit. It all belongs to God.

6. **Love is respectful and courteous of others.** Guys, this sounds like being a gentleman; and girls—before you "amen"—this sounds like being a lady, as well.

3 DAILY HABITS TO GROW IN
YOUR RELATIONSHIP WITH GOD

Habits make or break us. In fact, our lives are byproducts of the daily habits we form. Research has said it takes 21 days to form a habit. Take the next 3 weeks to build these 3 habits in your life, and watch your walk with God grow.

1. At breakfast each morning, read one chapter of Proverbs. By the time you're done eating, you will have easily read a chapter.

2. Find one Scripture in the chapter you read that really stands out to you. Write it down on a piece of paper or a 3 x 5 index card and carry it with you wherever you go.

3. Whenever you hit slow times in your day, such as being stuck in traffic on the school bus, pull out the card and meditate on your Scripture.

Commit these 3 simple habits to your life, and you will grow rapidly.

[MONEY MONOPOLY]

3 REASONS YOU SHOULD TITHE

There are really more than 3 reasons you should tithe; but if these don't inspire you to tithe, another 100 reasons won't either.

1. God says if you don't, you're robbing Him. (Mal. 3:10-11.) This doesn't sound like a very good plan. I'm sure God has a good security system that lets Him know anytime a thief robs Him of His tithes. Do you think God is going to bless a thief who is robbing Him?

2. God said that if you do what He says, He will flood you with blessings. It sounds like a good thing to be flooded with blessings. Get your boat ready for God's good flood.

3. God will work His pest control on anything that will try to attack your finances. Some people lose great financial crops because of pests, accidents, theft, and so forth. Use pest control by tithing.

God says, "Test me in this" (Mal. 3:10 NIV). Put Him to the test. Honor Him with your tithes, and watch the blessings flow your way.

5 MONEY VERSES TO COMMIT TO MEMORY

Romans 10:17 says faith comes by hearing God's Word. When you are under financial attack or feeling discouraged, you need to stand strong in faith. If you have these 5 Scriptures committed to memory, you can speak them and faith will come.

1. **Philippians 4:19 NIV:** "And my God will meet all your needs according to his glorious riches in Christ Jesus."

2. **Matthew 6:33 NIV:** "But seek first his kingdom and his righteousness, and all these things will be given to you as well."

3. **Luke 6:38 NIV:** "Give, and it will be given to you. A good measure, pressed down, shaken together and running over, will be poured into your lap. For with the measure you use, it will be measured to you."

4. **Deuteronomy 8:18 NIV:** "But remember the Lord your God, for it is he who gives you the ability to produce wealth."

5. **Galatians 6:7 NIV:** "Do not be deceived: God cannot be mocked. A man reaps what he sows."

Joshua 1:8 NIV says, "Do not let this Book of the Law depart from your mouth. Meditate on it day and night, so that you may be careful to do everything written in it. Then you will be prosperous and successful." Good advice!

4 WARNINGS JESUS GAVE ABOUT MONEY

Jesus taught many things about money. In His teachings, He shared the heavenly Father's plan for provision and prosperity; but He also gave some very stern warnings. Four warnings He gave are also important for us today. Listen, and avoid many problems. Ignore them, and face the consequences.

1. **Matthew 6:19** NIV: **"**Do not store up for yourselves treasures on earth, where moth and rust destroy, and where thieves break in and steal." This doesn't mean we don't save money, but rather that we don't put all our hope in money here. We should be wise and give generously to His kingdom, and we will have riches in heaven as well.

2. **Matthew 6:24** NIV: "No one can serve two masters. Either he will hate the one and love the other, or he will be devoted to the one and despise the other. You cannot serve both God and Money." You must choose whom your focus will be on—God or money. You can't be devoted to both.

3. **Matthew 6:25** NIV: "Therefore I tell you, do not worry about your life...." Worry robs us of joy, faith, and

time. It never produces good fruit. Trust God to provide for you.

4. **Matthew 13:22** tells us not to let the deceitfulness of wealth choke out our love for God and His Word.

Take heed to these warnings, and you will do well.

7 REWARDS OF THE GIVER

If you think you get the short end of the deal by being a giver, think again. Take a look at these 7 rewards Scripture promises to those who give.

1. You will prosper. (Prov. 1:25.) That's much better than the alternative.

2. You will be refreshed and encouraged by other people. (Prov. 11:25.) We all need this at different points in our lives.

3. You will get back what you give, but it will come back bigger and better. (Luke 6:38.)

4. God personally sees to it that you receive your reward. (Eph. 6:8.)

5. You will be flooded with good things. (Mal. 3:10.)

6. You will have supernatural protection over your finances. (Mal. 3:11.)

7. You will have treasure in heaven that no one can take away. (Luke 18:22.)

Take advantage of the rewards available to you by being a giver. You can watch others be blessed, or you can obey God's Word and receive blessings too.

3 BIBLE PERSONALITIES WHO WERE RICH

We often have the wrong idea that if we are going to sell out to Jesus, we must brace ourselves for a life of poverty. However, the opposite is true. When you see people in the Bible who surrendered their lives to God, you see them richly blessed beyond their wildest expectations.

1. Abraham obeyed God and left his homeland of Ur to follow God. He became very wealthy in livestock, silver, and gold (Gen. 13:2). He also became a great nation (Gen. 12:2).

2. Solomon, King David's son, chose to follow God at a very young age and asked God for wisdom. God was pleased with his request and gave him wisdom and great riches. (1 Kings 3:10-13.) His palace took 13 years to build; it was a beautiful crib. (1 Kings 7.) People came from all over the world to see Solomon's wealth and hear his wisdom. (1 Kings 10.)

3. Contrary to popular belief, Jesus was financially blessed. He had a full-time staff of 12 He took care of. He had an accountant named Judas (not a really honest one) to handle the money. We know He dressed

nicely because Roman soldiers gambled over His clothes at the cross.

Obey God, follow His Word, and you too can be financially prosperous.

[THE REWARDS

OF WORK]

5 THINGS GOD SAYS ABOUT WORK

Our work is very important to God. Unfortunately, there are a lot of teenagers who don't even think seriously about work until they get out of high school or even college, but now is the time to develop good work habits in your life. A strong work ethic will virtually ensure success in any career you choose.

Here are 5 critical things God's Word has to say about work.

1. If you don't work, you won't eat. (2 Thess. 3:10.) Work is the exchange God has created for all of us to gain finances to provide for our daily needs. God didn't say to pray, hope, or beg—He said to work.

2. We are to work as if our bosses were Jesus—not human beings. (Eph. 6:5.) Even when the boss isn't looking, the Lord sees all that you do.

3. Our work should produce good fruit and results. (Col. 1:10.) Don't just put in the time, but learn how to get results.

4. If we're faithful and consistent in the small things in our jobs, we'll be promoted to bigger tasks and responsibilities. (Matt 25:23.)

5. A worker is worthy of one's pay. (Matt. 10:10.) You should be paid fairly for your work; and once you've agreed on a wage, you have no right to complain about your pay. Be cheerful!

4 KINDS OF PEOPLE WHO
CONSTANTLY GET FIRED

I have been in the workforce for more than 20 years and have never been fired from a job. Unfortunately, along the way, I have seen many others who worked alongside me suffer this difficult experience. Most of the time, they had no one but themselves to blame. Many of these people fall into one of the following 4 categories:

1. **Those who cannot receive instruction or correction.** Instead of acknowledging their shortcomings and making the appropriate changes, they overflow with pride and refuse to listen.

2. **Those who cause strife in the team.** They may be talented and diligent workers, but they allow jealousy, competitiveness, and hunger for power to sabotage their abilities.

3. **Those who refuse to continue to grow and improve.** These people accept mediocrity and will not pay the price to increase their knowledge and ability to perform at their highest level.

4. **Those who are not truthful.** No matter how talented a person is, the individual cannot help an organization if he or she cannot be trusted.

3 REASONS YOUR RELATIONSHIP WITH YOUR PARENTS WILL AFFECT YOUR CAREER

Your relationship with your parents is simply preparation for the rest of your life, including your work and career. There are at least 3 important reasons your career will either succeed or fail as a direct result of how you get along with the authority in your house.

1. If you can't honor and obey those who love you in your home, it's unlikely you'll behave any better with a boss who won't be nearly as likely to forgive. Remember, your parents will be the last bosses you have who can't fire you.

2. Your parents have already been where you are headed. They have experienced the real world. If you're smart, you'll ask questions, listen to their experiences and wisdom, and learn what it takes to succeed.

3. There will be times when school, chores, and life at home will seem boring and redundant. The day will come when you will experience the same feelings with your job and career. Learning to persevere and rejuvenate your passion will put you ahead of the pack.

7 REWARDS OF A DILIGENT WORKER

Many people seek to do the least they possibly have to at a job. What they fail to understand is that they are blocking the blessings of God from coming their way. Proverbs 21:5 assures us that the plans of the diligent will lead to plenty, while those who are hasty in their work will find poverty. Here are 7 rewards of the diligent worker.

1. **Promotion.** Hard work will be rewarded with higher positions of responsibility.

2. **Recognition.** A diligent person will stand out from the crowd, acknowledged by many.

3. **Wealth.** Companies and organizations will pay good money to those who do their job well.

4. **Respect.** You will gain esteem from your friends, your family, your peers, and your community.

5. **Opportunity.** You will find yourself becoming very valuable to others who will open new doors for you to walk through.

6. **Influence.** You will earn the privilege of teaching, training, and mentoring those who will want to learn from your success.

7. **Fulfillment.** You'll never have to live with regrets, wondering what you could have accomplished if you had only given your best.

5 QUALITIES OF A VALUABLE EMPLOYEE

I currently have about 20 full-time employees and interns who serve under my direction and leadership. Each one of them is extremely important and valuable in contributing to our youth ministry. Here are the 5 qualities that make workers valuable.

1. **Diligent.** They give you 100 percent of their effort 100 percent of the time.

2. **Smart.** They think as they work, always coming up with better ways to get the job done more effectively.

3. **Faithful.** They will take just as much pride in and give as much attention to the small details of their work as they do big things.

4. **Loyal.** They speak well of you, fellow employees, and the organization to others and always seek what is best for the organization.

5. **Productive.** They get results, are careful with the finances, and help the organization grow.

[BECOME A

MONEY CHANNEL]

3 REASONS GOD WANTS YOU TO BE A CHANNEL

Webster's Dictionary defines a channel as "the course that anything moves through or past."[1] If you are willing to become a channel, God will be able to trust you with wealth and possessions. Too many Christians become wells instead of channels, holding on to what they get, refusing to allow their blessings to flow to others. So here are 3 reasons God is looking for you to be His channel.

1. **As a channel for blessings, you will reflect God's character.** God's very essence is to give. John 3:16 says that He so loved that He gave. When you give is when you are most like God.

2. **As a channel, you will see no limit to what God can bring your way.** When the Lord knows He can trust you to obey Him with all your provision, you are unlimited in your potential.

3. **A channel is always left with the residue of whatever comes through it.** Even as you obey God in giving, He will see that you continue to be blessed in the process.

3 KEYS THAT WILL OPEN
THE WINDOWS OF HEAVEN

In the Old Testament book of Malachi, God makes a promise to all His children. When we obey Him in the giving of our income, He will open the windows of heaven and pour out such blessings that there will not be room enough to receive them. (Mal. 3:8-12.) That means you will always have more than you need so that you can pass on your blessings to others as well. Here are 3 keys to getting those windows open in your life.

1. Bring in your tithes and offerings consistently. Your tithe is one-tenth of your income or paycheck from where you work. Your offering is over and above the 10 percent that is given in some way to extend God's kingdom.

2. He says to put your tithe and offerings in the storehouse so there will be food in His house. God's house today is His church. Your tithe belongs to your local church that you attend. Your offering can go to any Gospel-preaching church or ministry that you see bearing good fruit.

3. He tells you to prove Him with your obedience. To prove Him means to put Him to the test, expecting Him to come through. This simply means to use your faith when you give, believing that He will meet your needs and desires.

7 PROMISES GUARANTEED TO EVERY GIVER

When you obey God in the giving of your finances, you step into a special part of God's covenant with you. Giving consistently moves you into a new realm of supernatural provision. Here are 7 promises that will be yours if you give.

1. There is a harvest on the way back for every financial seed you plant. (2 Cor. 9:10.)

2. All of your needs will be met. (Phil. 4:19.)

3. You will have an abundance to give even more in the future. (2 Cor. 9:7,8.)

4. The devourer (Satan) will be rebuked over your life and possessions by God Himself. (Mal. 3:11.)

5. Spiritual fruit (souls of men and women) will abound to your heavenly bank account, which means you will reap extra rewards in eternity. (Phil. 4:17.)

6. You will receive back in direct proportion to the generosity of your gift. (2 Cor. 9:6.)

7. People who associate with you will have a supernatural, God-given desire to want to bless and assist you in every way. (Luke 6:38.)

5 THINGS TO BELIEVE GOD
FOR AS A TEENAGER

When you give to God, never give with spiritual apathy. As you give, you are sowing financial seed. Any good farmer expects and looks for a harvest after he's worked hard to plant his seed. Don't give and then walk away from your harvest. Believe God! Trust God! Look for that harvest to come. Here are 5 things to start believing God for right now.

1. **Believe God for the right husband or wife.** You can't just "claim" someone who doesn't really like you, but you can ask and trust God for the right one to come at the right time.

2. **Believe God for the right job, right now.** God will give you work right now and help you to earn extra money if you'll ask Him.

3. **Believe God for the right career in the future.** Trust God to lead you into your divine calling and occupation.

4. **Believe God for a good running vehicle.** You're soon going to need your own transportation. He will help you get it!

5. **Believe God for your education to be complete.** Whether it be high school, college, university, or other vocational training, trust Him to meet the need to get it.

5 WAYS YOU CAN GIVE
WITHOUT USING MONEY

While giving in other ways will never replace God's instructions to give financially, there are other very practical, tangible ways we can give. So keep giving in your finances, but start thinking of other ways to give of yourself as well. Here are some ideas to get you started.

1. Serve in your local church. You may be a greeter, usher, or prayer worker, but do something.

2. Look for opportunities to help people in your daily life. It may be assisting someone whose car has broken down on the side of the road or helping up a child who has fallen. Look for ways to be a blessing.

3. Offer to serve at a mission for the poor during the holidays, such as Thanksgiving and Christmas:

4. Take a week's vacation or part of your summer vacation and go on a mission trip.

5. Write a letter or make a telephone call to someone who has made an investment in your life. Let the person know how much you love and appreciate him or her.

[WHO WANTS TO BE

A MILLIONAIRE?]

5 OBSTACLES YOU MUST OVERCOME
TO GROW FINANCIALLY

The Bible is clear that God delights in the prosperity of His servants. (Ps. 35:27.) Yet many of His children do not prosper in the area of their finances. They have allowed at least 1 of 5 major obstacles to stand in their way of financial success.

1. **Fear.** Perhaps our greatest enemy is fear. Satan is the author of all fear, and too many Christians are afraid to take simple steps of faith with their money.

2. **Doubt.** Many Christians believe God wants to bless others, but not them. Faith comes by hearing and hearing by the Word of God (Rom. 10:17), so speak God's Word boldly concerning your money.

3. **Laziness.** You will not gain in your finances if you do not have a diligent hand. You must work hard for God to bless you.

4. **Arrogance.** First Peter 5:5 says that God resists the proud. God will resist blessing you if you remain proud and unwilling to be taught.

5. **Greed.** If you are constantly grabbing and hold everything you get with a tight fist, then you will block His future provision.

4 PRACTICAL THINGS YOU CAN DO
TO LEARN HOW TO MAKE MONEY

Growing in your ability to make money starts on the spiritual side. You listen to God, obey Him in tithes and offerings, and keep your heart focused on Him. There are also some practical things you must discover along the way. Here are 4 important things you can do to learn more.

1. Find a successful businessperson in your church and ask the individual to take 2 or 3 one-hour meetings to mentor you.

2. Read books and listen to audio programs by proven, successful experts in the field of finances, investments, and budgeting.

3. Ask some businesspeople in your church to recommend a quality financial advisor or broker you can meet with. This person will help you understand how to save and invest wisely in the stock market.

4. Find a good friend who has an interest in finances and investing. "Iron sharpens iron" (Prov. 27:17 NIV), so share and discuss the things you are learning together.

7 COMMON DENOMINATORS OF
THOSE WHO GROW RICH

The book *The Millionaire Next Door* documents that 80 percent of America's millionaires are first-generation rich.[2] That means that they did not inherit their money but earned it on their own. This book, and many others like it, tell us there are 7 common denominators of those who have grown wealthy.

1. They spend much less than what they earn at work.

2. They are careful and strategic in putting their time, energy, and money to work in fruitful ways.

3. Their parents were not always there for them to be bailed out when in financial trouble.

4. They carefully selected the right job in a career they enjoyed.

5. They learned how to market and advertise their own abilities and products.

6. They teach their children to grow up financially self-sufficient.

7. They believe that being good stewards of their money is more important than buying things to show status with others.

3 PLACES FOR SUCCESSFUL INVESTING

In order to grow your money, you are going to have to plant it like a seed in the right soil for it to produce. You must be willing to start small and take one simple step at a time. Remember, the steps (not the running leaps) of a righteous man are ordered of the Lord. (Prov. 37:23.) Here are 3 places you can successfully invest your money.

1. **In your own business.** This may be the best return you will ever get, because you have complete control over all that you do. It may be investing in lawn care equipment for a landscaping business. It could be an investment in a university to become a doctor.

2. **In the stock market.** When you buy stocks, bonds, or mutual funds (collections of stocks), you are basically buying a small part of a company like Wal-Mart, GAP, or General Motors. You must do very good research, get sound advice from experts, and believe that the stock you buy will grow. Remember this: 9 out of 10 companies fail in 5 years. Of those that survive the first 5 years, 9 out of 10 eventually fail as well.[3] So invest in proven companies that you know will be around a long time.

3. **In a home.** As soon as you can, buy a home after you get out of high school. While your cars and video games will depreciate, a home purchased in the right place at the right price will go up in value.

10 KEY QUESTIONS FOR SPENDING WISELY

The Bible promises that if we honor God with our possessions and first fruits (the tithe), our barns will be filled with plenty. (Prov. 3:9,10.) In the Old Testament, the barn is a storehouse of savings. If you are going to save effectively, you must spend wisely. Remember, it's not how much you make that counts but how much you have left over when it's all said and done. So here are 10 questions to consider before buying something.

1. Do I really need it?

2. Is the price right?

3. Is it the right time to buy?

4. Is there a substitute for this?

5. Is there any major disadvantage in this purchase?

6. Have I researched the item carefully?

7. Will its value increase/decrease dramatically?

8. Does it compliment my Christian testimony?

9. Does it require great expenses in upkeep?

10. Have I sought outside counsel?

[BUDGET, PLAN,

AND PROSPER]

4 DO'S AND 3 DON'TS OF BUDGETING

Budgeting your money is simply sitting down and making out a list of how much income you have versus how much you're paying out in bills and expenses each month. Your expenses include everything from clothing and gasoline to insurance and entertainment. This helps you to know "the state of your flocks," as Proverbs teaches us. (Prov. 27:23 NKJV.)

Here are 4 Do's:

1. Do be realistic about how much things cost. (Don't underestimate.)

2. Do pay the tithe first; this will ensure that the other 90 percent is protected.

3. Do pay yourself second. As a rule, putting 10 percent into savings or investments is good.

4. Do eliminate as much debt, interest, and unnecessary luxuries as possible.

Here are 3 Don'ts:

1. Don't finance purchases on a credit card unless you intend to pay the full amount (no interest) on the due date.

2. Don't put yourself in a financial straight jacket, having every last penny spoken for.

3. Don't be afraid to ask someone for help in your planning if you're having trouble making ends meet.

7 STEPS TO EFFECTIVE PLANNING

Proverbs 21:5 NKJV tells us, "The plans of the diligent lead surely to plenty." It's good to be a diligent worker, but that is not enough. You must also be a good planner. As the saying goes, "If you fail to plan, you are planning to fail." Check out these steps to becoming a good planner.

1. Keep a personal calendar, writing down plans, goals, and deadlines regularly.

2. As you make your plans, remain flexible to allow the Lord to give you counsel, making adjustments along the way. (Prov. 19:21.)

3. As you plan, seek counsel from those around you whom you know well and trust. (Prov. 15:22.)

4. Plans without deadlines are just dreams. Give yourself realistic dates to accomplish each stage of your plan.

5. Write your plan down in a personal journal, referring back to it regularly for inspiration and focus. (Hab. 2:2.)

6. Don't try to do it alone. Recruit the help and support you need to pull the plan off.

7. Never, ever give up. Persistence is the greatest quality of successful people.

6 KEYS TO GETTING THE
MOST OUT OF YOUR TIME

Time is a commodity that can never be replaced. If you lose money or a possession, you can always get it back. But once you turn 16, you will never be 15 again! The Bible tells us to "redeem," or make the very most of, the time we have. (Eph. 5:16.) Here's how:

1. Appreciate the value of your time. You only get 86,400 seconds a day. Use them well.

2. Set priorities. Remember these words from Zig Ziglar: "You can't do everything you want to do, but you can do anything you want to do."[4]

3. Plan your daily and weekly schedule. Write it down.

4. Don't allow unnecessary interruptions and time-wasters to steal valuable time from your projects.

5. Politely hang up on telemarketers!

6. Learn to delegate things that other people can and will do for you. You can't create more time, but you can use the time of others.

7 BOOKS THAT CAN CHANGE YOUR LIFE

Here are 7 books that contain powerful truths and ideas that, when applied, have the potential to change your future. Although most of these are not necessarily Christian books, each of them contains powerful biblical principles. Don't buy and read them all at once, but start checking them out one at a time.

1. *Sam Walton—Made in America* by Sam Walton: the inspiring story of a regular guy who built Wal-Mart.

2. *The 7 Habits of Highly Effective People* by Steven Covey: a bestseller for many years.

3. *Developing the Leader Within You* by John Maxwell: a guide to moving up the leadership ladder.

4. *The Millionaire Next Door* by Thomas J. Stanley and William D. Danko: the surprising secrets of America's wealthy.

5. *Rich Dad—Poor Dad* by Robert T. Kiyosaki: what the rich teach their kids about money that the poor and middle class do not.

6. *The Heart of a Leader* by Ken Blanchard: insights on the art of influence.

7. *How to Win Friends and Influence People* by Dale Carnegie: keys to winning in your relationships with people.

3 STEPS FOR MONEY MULTIPLICATION

The Bible promises to multiply the financial seeds we sow. I want to give you a 3-step plan to multiply your money. Multiplication is a math exercise. I believe in order to get to this level, you must first go through 3 other math exercises with your finances. Here they are:

1. **Addition.** It's the simplest form of math. You must be faithful to add all that you can to your success before God will step in to do His part. Add your work, your planning, your prayer, and your persistence—and good things will follow.

2. **Subtraction.** Hebrews 12:1 says to lay aside every weight and sin that sets us back. We must discipline ourselves to subtract and take out destructive habits and sin, which will stop us from inheriting all the blessings of God.

3. **Division.** You must divide, organize, and diversify your abilities and money. In other words, "Don't put all your eggs in one basket." Genesis 13:2 says Abraham was rich in livestock, silver, and gold. He had several

channels through which God could bless him. So do you. Ask Him to show you what they are!

ENDNOTES

[1] *Webster's New World College Dictionary,* 3d Edition. New York: McMillian Company, s.v. "channel."

[2] Stanley, Thomas J., Ph.D., and William D. Danko. *The Millionaire Next Door.* Pocket Books, 2000, p. 3.

[3] Kiyosaki, Robert T. *Rich Dad—Poor Dad.* Warner Books, 2000, p. 82.

[4] Ziglar, Zig. *Top Performance—How to Develop Excellence in Yourself and Others,* Berkley Publishing Group, 1991.

MEET BLAINE BARTEL

Past: Came to Christ at age 16 on the heels of the Jesus movement. While in pursuit of a professional freestyle skiing career, answered God's call to reach young people. Developed and hosted groundbreaking television series *Fire by Nite*. Planted and pastored a growing church in Colorado Springs.

Present: Serves under his pastor and mentor of nearly 20 years, Willie George, senior pastor of 12,000-member Church on the Move in Tulsa, Oklahoma. Youth pastor of Oneighty®, America's largest local church youth ministry, and reaches more than 1,500 students weekly. National director of Oneighty's® worldwide outreaches, including a network of over 400 affiliated youth ministries. Host of Elevate, one of the largest annual youth leadership training conferences in the nation. Host of *Thrive*™, youth leader audio resource series listened to by thousands each month.

Passion: Summed up in 3 simple words: "Serving America's Future." Life quest is "to relevantly introduce the person of Jesus Christ to each new generation of young people, leaving footprints for future leaders to follow."

Personal: Still madly in love with his wife and partner of 20 years, Cathy. Raising 3 boys who love God, Jeremy—17, Dillon—15, and Brock—13. Avid hockey player and fan, with a rather impressive Gretzky memorabilia collection.

To contact Blaine Bartel,

write:

Blaine Bartel

Serving America's Future

P.O. Box 691923

Tulsa, OK 74169

www.blainebartel.com

Please include your prayer requests
and comments when you write.

To contact Oneighty®, write:

Oneighty®

P.O. Box 770

Tulsa, OK 74101

www.Oneighty.com

OTHER BOOKS BY BLAINE BARTEL

Ten Rules to Youth Ministry and Why Oneighty®
Breaks Them All

every teenager's
Little Black Book
on sex and dating

every teenager's
Little Black Book
on cool

every teenager's
Little Black Book
of hard to find information

PRAYER OF SALVATION

A born-again, committed relationship with God is the key to a victorious life. Jesus, the Son of God, laid down His life and rose again so that we could spend eternity with Him in heaven and experience His absolute best on earth. The Bible says, "For God so loved the world, that he gave his only begotten Son, that whosoever believeth in him should not perish, but have everlasting life" (John 3:16).

It is the will of God that everyone receive eternal salvation. The way to receive this salvation is to call upon the name of Jesus and confess Him as your Lord. The Bible says, "That if thou shalt confess with thy mouth the Lord Jesus, and shalt believe in thine heart that God hath raised him from the dead, thou shalt be saved. For whosoever shall call upon the name of the Lord shall be saved" (Romans 10:9,13).

Jesus has given salvation, healing, and countless benefits to all who call upon His name. These benefits can be yours if you receive Him into your heart by praying this prayer:

> *Heavenly Father, I come to You admitting that I*
> *am a sinner. Right now, I choose to turn away*
> *from sin, and I ask You to cleanse me of all*

unrighteousness. I believe that Your Son, Jesus, died on the cross to take away my sins. I also believe that He rose again from the dead so that I may be justified and made righteous through faith in Him. I call upon the name of Jesus Christ to be the Savior and Lord of my life. Jesus, I choose to follow You, and I ask that You fill me with the power of the Holy Spirit. I declare right now that I am a born-again child of God. I am free from sin, and full of the righteousness of God. I am saved in Jesus' name, amen.

If you have prayed this prayer to receive Jesus Christ as your Savior, or if this book has changed your life, we would like to hear from you. Please write us at:

Harrison House Publishers

P.O. Box 35035

Tulsa, Oklahoma 74153

You can also visit us on the Web at

www.harrisonhouse.com

Additional copies of this book
are available from your local bookstore.

HARRISON HOUSE
Tulsa, Oklahoma 74153

THE HARRISON HOUSE VISION

Proclaiming the truth and the power
Of the Gospel of Jesus Christ
With excellence;

Challenging Christians to
Live victoriously,
Grow spiritually,
Know God intimately.